Names of Blessing

PIER GIORGIO DI CICCO

NOVALIS

© 2009 Novalis Publishing Inc.

Cover design and layout: Blair Turner
Cover photograph and interior photographs: Pier Giorgio Di Cicco

Business Offices:
Novalis Publishing Inc.
10 Lower Spadina Avenue, Suite 400
Toronto, Ontario, Canada
M5V 2Z2

Novalis Publishing Inc.
4475 Frontenac Street
Montréal, Québec
Canada H2H 2S2

Phone: 1-800-387-7164
Fax: 1-800-204-4140
E-mail: books@novalis.ca

www.novalis.ca

Library and Archives Canada Cataloguing in Publication

Di Cicco, Pier Giorgio, 1949-
  Names of blessing / Pier Giorgio Di Cicco.

Poems. ISBN 978-2-89646-124-0

  1. Christian poetry, Canadian (English). I. Title.

PS8557.I248 N34 2009   C811'.54   C2009-900909-9

Printed in Canada.

Some of the poems included in this collection were first published by the *Catholic Register* and the *Toronto Star*, and broadcast by the Canadian Broadcasting Corporation.

We acknowledge the financial support of the Government of Canada through the Book Publishing Industry Development Program (BPIDP) for our publishing activities.

5 4 3 2 1 13 12 11 10 09

Acknowledgments

There are many names of blessing, and they include Fr. Joseph Dal Ferro, Monsignor Robert Nusca, Margaret Reel, Cal Brook, Patricia McCarney, Anne McIlroy, Teresa Sorrentino, Andy Vergalito, Carolyn Taylor, Francesco Lorrigio, John Bentley-Mays, Vaclav and Cristina Vaca, Rudy Wietfeldt and Ted Tyndorf. In appreciation for countless fraternal graces, these poems are dedicated to Mario Romano.

Contents

I

II

III

IV

I

Songsters

Here I am singing, writing as you
bequeath, behest, demand with teeth
like dandelions, up the side of brook and
wall and tears and laugh
down the trickle of my inside that is
name, like me, of dust.

Is it the coyote
Is it faith or chance,
Is it my arm made of blood or just pining
and wishing that makes me lean towards you like
planet for the moon, like this and that,
like rhetoric, like plush fruit for
maw of inarticulate man?

I love you like myself.
I will go small like a grief
unto mine eyes that Your hands are,

singing and writing and dancing into the grave
that is beauty and music.

Cavern and marmoset have Your spelling too,
whom I will whisper to. We are strings and violin
for what won't play out in the stars; man and
meditating things, blood and arc of His
love.

A Dying Friend

His eyes fell out of his head so full of
pain and stunned with it,
and Christ too came visiting and found his
head vacant, whereupon I placed a cross in
his hands and spit a kiss moon-wise, his wife
straddling two stars, his children star-dust.

What is this man I said but a friend
And shadow stitched to me,

Whom I will follow like shoes all the
Weary days of my life.

Some days he was on the planet, like all of us
And then searched for the saviour between beads
Of sweat.

What poetry comes out of him like a child,
And all the words, like mama

That I lather my heart in,
As I say goodbye

And ask him for the thief's name, as if my own.

Advent

We are all waiting to be
Home. Between the stars, and trees,
And byways, the promise
Of arrival. How shall we be there,
But by the depth of hunger,
When everything looked similar to
Him, the mistaken groom?

The innocence of the child is like
The wide-eyed world wanting its
Owner.

We are tired of being stewards
Of waiting. This time we will take each light
For what it is, a window, a kiss, a wink
When all eternity eavesdrops on
The lonely heart.

I do not know which moves faster,
The end of time coming toward us
Or every act sounding like our eager
Care for what comes for us—

Jesus, never letting us alone
As if to soothe his brow by every name
He loves.

Angels of Christmas

You are the angel I gave to a child.
You come back to me, though I thought I'd
lost you. It was not the angel of foreboding
and conclusions as I'd thought. It was not
the angel pointing earthward, or inward or
in any direction. You were the angel of love and pain,
or rather, simply the angel of the obvious
always escaping—that angels are made of the
little bit they pick up on earth and the
silken feathers of above. They are the marrying
point of pain and love, of sacrifice and wonder.
I know you now when I buy you in porcelain
or bronze, in brightening crystal and lead, or
marbled like my eyes, slated for Christ.
I know you now and hope to see you in
all things without wings.
There are no wise men. You are the
days of our lives following the wounded
hope, the wizened and beleaguered—those who
follow their sorrow to the ends of the earth
for an answer and see only themselves in
the night sky, mercy marrying the lust for God;
and the bandaged, ruined feet—coming to a manger
to find more of ourselves, newly innocent
as the clockwork of the skies.
You do not fool me, angels; you see with my eyes
what I would see with grace; my self denuded
and radiant-hearted, and the star of Bethlehem
carried in Kansas, Peoria, Illinois, and places
far and away from me, brought to His care.

Biography

Let's see, I was born a wisp of a gentleness on
one side of the Atlantic, and brought up among
Appalachians. That done, there is always
a misery in a story, belonging to a cloud
as I went through the
hearts of men as if they minded it.
Today I meet a man in the middle of the hellhole. He says:
"I pray the Lord see you out of your grief,
whatever it may be". I bless him. We embrace, for
nothing is lonely
unless it is unforgiven. His words are water
for me to drink, and it pours through
our hearts like a river through a canyon.
I will pray for that man,
for we will both lie in the ground,
reclaimed by innocence.
Soon, I shall rail for one last time, at sky and
happenstance, and unearth myself from grief,
for we are all a resurrection by dying.
And I will move away from the land
that seeks to bury me
as I walk with a heavy heart,
that I release now, like
a bird, called heavenly.

Blue Jay Scamper

Thank you for this day
in which I am not dead

but figuring
how to be in a hostile world
by an act of faith.

Thank you then for ageing sunlight
and dandelions that look northward to my eyes

and for the plain look of me.

Between gratitude and peacelessness I sally,
abandoning one music for another.

Though I seek to be safe in
the furniture of the world,
I wish to speak
your heart;

to know simply
Your presence
among us.

I Suddenly Realize

I suddenly realize who I am, a
poised boy for the stars;

between blades of grass,
I deign to greet Him like dew or air things,
so light as butterflies or words.

I am like dew too, waiting for Him to
soak me like clouds, their lining,
like breath which is wind, like the inside palm
of Him on the brow of the planet.

I am, myself, this hunger of what dropped
of his creating, of Himself, like
joy left for picking,

wanting company, of Himself,
and calling in the wood "find me", like everything.

And here I am, acknowledgement like sunrise,
or a plain man thanking
what must be His, and made.

Mercy

I killed two bats,
and went blind;

for having killed two bats, poor things,
like me, all heart, dumb; listening
like a bat now,
I remember how they crept away, or tried to,
how they flew at my face, scared
in their flight.

all the dumb things
I have killed that knew me, all the things I was like—
grass, leaves—I have gnashed
at all manner of things I
was not man enough to mirror.

gently now, I treat things,
and lift my
face to clouds as if
to bless.

Poem for the Madonna

sunrise be yours, red rays
my entire life.
… birds, chipmunks …
the world as you knew it,
wished for, prayed for,

this day betrothed to
its mistakes, this yellow skin,
all unremembered things.

bless
the waters of the Susquehanna,
picnics in lonely towns,
galaxies,
coronas,
my hands folded

and angels that wander
through my bones like
revelation.

True Language

My grief has been
nothing commensurate to
joy, except for words that
wound my body
as argument to God,
as if to see myself
were to justify
Him;

my grief might
explain love, why flowers
balk at nothing, what might be
trees and what demands
being heard,

by Him, who makes

my body braille for
what is unpronounceable—
His passion.

Blind

she is blind. sits on the
veranda under the catalpa tree
remembering 80 years, maybe,
as blood and leaf-wind.
she looks as if she might be looking at me.
but I know she cannot see and yet
looks as if she sees me.
it is my soul looking for its
misses. she says what have you made of
anything you have, that I miss, that
I wish I had, with your eyes?
I am so happy saying a prayer for her,
like the wind that prays with her.
I hope in her head, she is happy and making peace with
the god of corpuscles and basic instincts
like a baby held in her arms in some year of her life.

I will move on from her,
like a homeless wanderer.
funny how home is only in the pitiful, for us,
who have everything to look forward to
like an illusion waiting for love.

Identity

the gentleness of the eyes on
a figurine
that I remember in my mother's hands;

it is a gentleness I have not found in temples
but in prayerful hands and syllables.

who knows what is cheek to cheek with
angels?
I hear
the flutter,

and my mother scampering across the lawn
with tiaras and light things made of
music boxes and songs she used to sing.

I am more part of the sky for this—
this gentleness that is

my only culture.

Myself the Beggar

But I want to go home now, and so I will park my car at the
Esso refinery at sunset by the lake, or just watch
aimless young people on some derelict corner thumbing their
nose at God for giving them nothing to do. I will go to
where people are not ugly but just lost between time and
promise. I want to go home, to images,
to homes I never had, like the homes of people's hearts
and knock, and watch the door swing open and, when they see
no one standing there, waft a kiss through the opening,
like a gift with no name on it.
For I am not me. I am no one. Emptied of all the burnt barns
I have been, of all the cremations, hurt past
all caring, like the man in the street,
happy to receive anything, taking a handout, and it feels
like a giving, as I reach out my hand to you,
my friend, stranger, benevolent one—
I hold my hand out, and whatever you put
in it, is yours.

Prayer of Finding

Here I will find Him,
in an alphabet of loon and otter.

And the impulse to go to mother
will be laid to rest like a child.

There is no need,
and I will respect the helping hand
when I am found.
But I will search nothing.

I am like a stone. I wait,
and dream of sunlight.

If only these arteries looked like
stone. They scream flowers
where the body has not forsaken me.

There is something I have not understood about
these arteries; how they are like waters in a canyon
carving out stone to make it look beautiful.

Blood, then, is for carving.
I am not stone. I am sleeping artisan.

I cannot carve myself into masterpiece,
but by the waters through somebody else's life,
I make a beautiful thought of fields and otter.
I am the poem my throat cannot make.

And my throat is not stone;
it is what sings like rain, as I have waited,

and the sunlight has arrived,
by something other than me,
and I am, like the loon and otter,

alphabet, and found.

The Earth Speaks

Images and images, of rushing tides,
and imagined swallowed islands, of the
earth's wobbled axis, of the flat hand of the
earth patting itself to wake conscience;

of the nuclear tests that rock
the cradle, of the awakened sleep
of a hundred countries to care for what
could not be cared about under one's nose—
the thought of death coming to anyone,
finally personal, while the thought of joy
starves in the streets.

This is the planet about to wonder
of itself; blood and wars measured against
the galactic random, wondering if
cosmic will speaks to earthly wishes;
what have we owed, that we have not paid up?
What is the debt of love?
And how many cruelties have answered
this many prayers?

Each death, unheard, has been the heart's casualty,
which now the earth makes public.

The Wilderness

the wilderness is about
making somebody happy
over and over again
is about good over evil
and so many other clichés;
it is about more than intelligence—
it is about the softest things having sway
over your life. is about moths and cats
and badgers, closing the door on no one.
it is about marrying yourself—

it is about rising above
any number of things, looking at yourself from above,
the landscapes of you, the mean trajectories,
the bumbling desires going door to door,
rising above and looking down and exonerating.

the greatest things—let's have an understanding—
are not confusing sensuality with passion,
of love with fulfilment,
of heaven with possibility; the greatest things
are about belonging to what you have no command over—
sunsets, tears, and the face that is dearest;
love is about being killed when you lack the inclination—

also;
moths, moths, moths, moths
and the fire, the fire is not hot, the fire is the beloved,
the fire is the legacy, from *legare*—
what ties the fabric of things together, human beings,
what you see between them, that makes
them sense to each other.

the wilderness is knowing this, with or without company.
the wilderness is the embers after the fire,
is nostalgia for what you have given, and grace before
what feeds you next; and the awful patience before God.

Alluding to Song

There is a kind of poem that God listens to; it has
to do with hunger, or the secret of the day,
a fly on a pane, yesterday's rabbit tracks.
The poem refused that may get used
not knowing
what will come of it,

the stone rejected,
the song He won't call song,
but a hand
unconscious of its need.

We are not fed by the right hand
and the poem without this arrogance
is the first phonetic
of star-gazing. The constellations do not
ask why we should love so much in
an orbit of skin and bones.

It is wonder—

this call
to be with Him,
like
stardust or woodscape,
where the otter feeds, and calls its
brothers, the
marmoset and sage.

II

Conversation with God

Here I am alone with you
again on a Friday afternoon
with the sun going down, being drawn down—
whatever you are doing with it, with your
puppetry, your masterful whatever;
What have you done to my heart? Pulled
the shutters on that too in my race
towards others? Today you keep it still,
as if you rested between the beats—
a moment of conversation within the heartbeats
your voice between every beat, saying,
"I love you I love you";
I am tired. You say "rest. Want nothing, need
no one. The flowers of those you love, hold them
up in your left hand", you tell me, like a flame,
like a tribute; like a sun that takes the
place of the one setting.

Driving Dark Roads

I love
that little trailer in the field,
and lights,
and rhythms and
coyotes.

I always
arrive at this trailer in the woods,
to make a butterfly of memories,
on the earth.

I watch with autumn eyes
the transcended leaf,

and the anointed planet.
And I will bless
a man of passion,

this gossamer and wing,
this town I come upon, this place,
myself.

Ash Wednesday

on Ash Wednesday it occurs to
me, I am poor in body and lug it like
a thing I use to clean the driveway with
as snowy ashes fall from heaven but
as snowflakes.

and I yearn to climb between those
snowflakes and find a bone
that makes the planet,
and its sundry beauty,

which does not fool me, presentiment that it is;
as I sing for the star maker my own futility,

like a madman needing love.

Dedication

I sing for you.
I am made for song.
It is my purpose, to invent new music, as a kind of prayer
that everything is, a cane tapping, a child running, the way
a leaf falls in its arpeggio. Everything states "consort",
"orchestration", and even music is to Him what is unrecognizable
to us:
the poor conversation, the bad day; it is our forcing
of a called tune that makes us deaf. For His musics weave
like wind, taking a sudden turn, holding up leaves, blowing the
snow.
We tap into his musics and call it a page, a song.
When our will is congruent to what we hear,
we are poets,
and people of prayer.

Grazia, the Fisherman

Brother Grazia died, without
saying goodbye.
Last time I saw him we
spoke of hands.
I weep for others
who died in our remorse.

The lake, without him;
the boat is empty.
His gestures unfinished,
I finish
and inhabit our laughter.

On the far side of the lake,
where the dragonflies skim the water,

the statues of saints
sleep in the alcoves of prayer.

Kenosis

If you take more from me,
so much that you have given
what should I do
but praise you?

What do,
but gather pine branches,
look at birds?
and if I cannot look at birds,
or move,
I will indelibly
scratch the cross onto my
oaken heart and free myself.

After vocabularies, timetables,
syllables
I will like wafting snow just
drift towards you,
and obey,
not by the hand that names me but
by the wind called spirit.

Mortality

You can write what you want, the blades
of grass still wait for you, and carry
your little cart of mother's cameos and things.
He will take them too. Let me
go into the yard, all bones of me,
and sing today.

For I will wait for God to finish what I cannot.

I hear him in everything.
It is so cool,
this deafened thing, myself, that writes,
like tendrils, like fingers,
what I would choke, like my own throat,
to have me warble,
like the sky, for Him—
melter of my dreams, melter of what
comes between us, like vellum earth.

Brides and Visitors

Today's the anniversary of my ordination
to the priesthood.
I haven't told my parishioners. They'd make such a fuss over me.

Someone sends me a prayer card from Baltimore.

I wink at Jesus as I leave the chapel door tonight—
four old ladies and a farmer who can't hold a note—

God has arranged for nobody to call.

Some twenty-five prayer books around me
screaming dead brethren and unwritten poems for
the saints and angels I have known.

Mainly, I wait for the angel of deafening love;
who will arrive on the stroke
of midnight.
I wait, like a bride.
so I can say
when he arrives: I've made
everything he gave me into a portent and a sign,
just to welcome Him home, to welcome Him home,
my tired angel, who has scoured the earth for me.

Taking up Residence

look at those snowflakes, Father,
why don't you make me one of them?
why don't you just make me a snowflake and
be done with it.

here in this new house
in the woods, away from past grief, I am

a map, with
no conscience.
I go from mirrors
to the evidence,
with no stories to remember,
a child that knows not to put his hand
to the fire.

why don't you make me a snowflake?
they fall and are forgotten.

make me of water
that runs into spring.

Let this place be a home
and
let the mirrors sing
of badger and moonrise
Let this place be yours
with
auspices, and blessing.

For My Mother on All Souls' Day

I nearly phoned you again today.
It was Halloween last night;
They were whooping it up on College St.
It's good you're underground at a little
country church I pray in.

Tomorrow is All Souls;
I still smoke. I found dad's transistor radio.
I have a new book I hope you liked; like the letter
you wrote
to God that I found yesterday.

I see you in glass mobiles that refract the
gracious sun at 5 pm; I feel your tidiness as I
move towards the fridge and get things done.
I am unfilled of the silence that was between us.

Let us build a house away from the whooping and things.
Let's say it's my heart, or ours; your fragile
bones anoint me—be they molecular in what I breathe.
Help me clean the rugs. May the telephone never ring
without the hope of love you put in me.
The days I almost phone you, let someone call
to have them hear your voice.

Loot Bag Heaven

I have looked into the house of
my happiness

and it is a warm dinner
with my friends, my limitations,
who meant no harm

and they hardly recognize an old man
staring in.

It is my heart barely making out
my features, it has been
so long since I left home,

with so little to report
and so eager
for a conversation with
the small boy,

the one still in my eyes.

People Without Money

people without money see things,
like fields and wheat;

firs and pines make their statement,
are heard.
Christmas lights are windows.
the new year is an old friend, not a scheme.

people without money are not rich in
anything but minutes

and a hello
beaten out of grief.

they do not build cities.
time uses them to build
indifferent
beauties.

they have this sad appetite that makes them
hungry for what has no place,
like the wash of a creek,
newspapers left behind.

they cannot be harvested.
they are what history cherishes,
redeems;

they do not inherit the earth,

but simply the world
without us.

Presbyteral Love

forget the strategies and pep talks.
open the doors to each other—
there is no ethnic component, no ministerial
genius
without welcome—
and it begins with one's own.

for the missions are not far away;
they are here,
and the solitude
and the pioneer gospel
are in the asphalt jungle.

family is not an abstraction
it is to be felt
before it is preached,
without protocol.

welcome and response—
the calling cards of Christ.

the polemic is in the water.
do not drink it.

the first kiss is to
stay human,
to persuade that the Savior is not
an administrator,
to persuade that love is antidote to wealth,
to persuade the brotherly.

Purpose

it is my "ethos", to live, in search, to marry like
a benediction my words and world, to have the world
belong to me, like I was always "hers".
to stitch the almost paradise to my fading skin,
in time for a bon voyage for transformation;
to just "belong", before everything has me.

to finish the duty of being placed on the planet,
by wishing well with
words that do the right thing and tag
love to trees and criminals.

this passion, about no paradise I knew,
but evocations of what might be if
I just round the corner with my throat intact
with someone willing to be named
as love.

The Homeless

He comes at me in sub-zero weather
and gestures madly, grunts and groans,
forms ovals with his mouth, holding up two fingers, three,
and finally points to the donut shop across the street.
He wants money for a coffee. I empty my pockets and he grunts
a thank you and sidles across the road with baggy pants and
old sneakers as I wonder at his whereabouts, where he lives, and
what might have brought him to where he is, on the planet in
winter.

He is me, grunting and groaning in my life.
I too make sounds
for any passerby to give me directions to the next bit of mercy;
the man is me, stunned under flourescent lights,
with huge fingers and a maw of a mouth that can't
explain him.

I call him my son, my life, or my brother.
Someone said to me today, "what goes out as heart,
comes back as heart".
Very well, he is my heart come back like an idiot
I must nurse; he is my screamings, my more articulate
screamings for love.

He is God in tatters for my taking.
He is much, and himself, whom I will never take home,
whom God visits since I cannot love.

He is my own shock
at my terrible need,
whom I cannot run away from, where once I might have;
because I have been bedfellows with my own
stinking grief, and now cannot scare myself away;
and so I make friends
with everything that looks like me,
impoverished wonder that I am,
with no facsimiles
to shun.

Waiting for Each Other to Die

It is betrayal that makes death look
unpalatable—
it wouldn't be so bad in a room
full of friends,
singing for each other as an
occurrence.

But when death is an empty
heart,
there is nothing more.

Here is some moonlight,
some small consolation,
a haystack in an empty field.

I scream
and I dream my courage; and will,
until my breath is taken from me.

Then I will dance and smile
with the angel that brings
earth to heaven
in the eyes of my friends,

bright with endurance.

Elegy for Brother Grigoire

In his
cell he had only a violin,
and crucifix,
a breviary.

He taught me
the sacristy linen and holy books,
and accepted
nothing in return.

He lies in the dark in the shrine.

One after the other
they lie there.
Raban, his aviator gloves,
Placidus, his one good eye.
Damasus and his beret,
Alex with his broken rosary.

They lie in the dark.

Upstairs, Anthony washes the floors
weeping among
crucifixes,
turning the lights off.

I do not attend these funerals.
Dragonflies and things
carry my prayers for the dead.

The crickets sing what is left of
my heart.

Christ in a Friend

there is this guy who is
as much like you as once in
a while in a lifetime you send along;
people whose benevolence and good
remind me of you at your best
(as if they didn't fail me at their worst).
A man whose integrity is hunger for you.
You should see how he works at making
You visible. He kisses theology with each
fall of sparrow.
I want you to have this guy live forever;
so I love him like the hunger in myself,
and there's the Christ.
Take me, rather than him, if you must.
Of course you don't, or then
you might. And may I not forget
the promise of your love.
Still, send him flowers and things,
and make me love my life
as much as he loves me.
There is this man who dresses plainly
with your love, showing up with jeans,
disheveled hair; like you,
uncamouflaged of
leaves and weather;
identifiable,
incarnate.

Trumpet

There is no news forthcoming
on the edge of my wilderness. I learn new
things as a final resort so He can see
me flitting on the planet, requisitioning home.

I want to play flowers and griefs and blue bells
and a handshake, I want to pour my breath
into the world like blessing.

I want the medium of song to be your eyes
as I look at them, your gentleness to be
arpeggio, the sky to be written in His quick hand,

before the night shuts us. I want
the angel of the new moon to
become any sparrow, and his music to be
light for the moths we are.

I want to shut my voice and become song,
transfigured, like grace coming to roost
on my ignorant head, for there is a heart in me
called love of man, and everyone hears it,

this music, deafening; this mouth called need of
humankind for God.

III

A Few Noticeable Things

the snow concocts its panorama
and there are other things I
love—let's say the shadow of the stems of
flowers against the wall,
a kitchen table lamp, a vase.

I wonder what they do, these world things,
blessed, in languages too subtle for me to hear
as if they were going somewhere—
blessed things, by my breath.

there is a kind of song I am
deaf to, like the place of death that is not death, the
melody I am not from, but must
be music of.

perhaps
that is all "perfecting" is,
giving earth new resonance by being a lyric
man beneath it.

so I sing these things by sunlight;
flowers, stems, and lamp, as dusk fades them into
what I cannot speak, unless I become subtle,
like humility, and
tone myself to the created, dark in my ignorance,
but bright for every morning thrust that
invents what is seen,
irrevocably.

Consolation for a Friend

God is speaking between the towers
of grass.
He says raindrops.
Marvelous. No time
for bitterness, sagas,
unforgiving.

Where did God go
between train trips,
infatuations, beneath the
sheets of skies, events and things
of seriousness we are?

There are
raindrops for the dying,
for farmers,
for poems and lovers.
He sends weather,
a lost lace doily,
and whatever your sparklers were,
a baby's eyes, the moon and friends.

If he has a song, it is this stillness
I send to you, like prayer that says:

don't let the stars hear you weeping.
There is rain and time enough
to lie exhausted in what He leaves for us—
our life, unended in his arms, and recollection
of plenty, doctored by His finger on
our eyes.

Disenchantment

We want, to live
like practicing for heaven,

and want to know what to
do with
desire—
the thing that's
not washed down;
and sick
of waking from it.
Is it real?

You want to sleep
away from desire,
and the screaming things—
the love, the tree, the shore, the
derelict heart of everything.

Wouldn't it be better to be
a parched leaf on
a country road in autumn?
To be useful, like a prayer,
while everything spins,
around, screeching, kissing?
To be an icon of happiness,
to catch like dew
some starlight;
to be still, and wonderful
and happy for something?

Landowner

The wilderness is the nightmare
you wake to;
you check the cupboards,
go to the window and
return to your conscience.
The nightmare is the man you were,
weeping at the goodness betrothed.
But the wilderness tolls at any hour
as the riders of judgement pass.

You move from the window
with a stone face.
The sun rises
between the portals of
what might have been,
what might have been forgiven
with one more
act of love.

And the shy animals come to the gate
and stand at the garden and the stream,
innocent of the hand that feeds them.

Remembering Griefs

As I sit by the river bank,
and watch the water and wonder,
the present is a tabernacle,
away from blow and dread.

I cannot be hurt now that I am older.
And vindication has led nowhere, like
the silted currents of the bay.

I have my life—
the one I always looked forward to,

and the promised land, whatever it was.
I have arrived.
and am free to plant the trees
and nurture the garden
while the fabric of hate unweaves.

Finally, I have come to forgive myself,
only to realize

I belong to
the world,
just to redeem it.

Residence

This is such a charming house.
Someone raised a family here,
kept it clean and tidy; it was love
that kept it well.
No ghosts, no haunting.
Someone was happy here.
Maybe I usher this place by my residence, from
the living to the dead, like everything else.
There is no life to be brought here. The lilacs will
bloom no matter what, the hawks fly in, the coyote,
nose his way curiously into the shed.
I am healed by the love the house knew,
or maybe I am imagining it.
Or I am all the love there is,
and the hopes I have buried
stir deep in the heart of the earth,
and the house is their blessing.

Shaking Hands After Church

you should see these faces,
in a glimpse
of earnest

in the 12 o'clock sun.
they file out into their lives,
suddenly themselves.

I subsist in their
trueness,

their courageous eyes
besieged by wrinkles and pain.

it is the wonder I live for;
their capable
wonder,

their words. God-sent.
some enliven, inspired by
sunlight, like gifts
from a fire-wheel.

who knows whose love is meant for whom?
you will be
bread for someone
or other.

what I see is
hope that outlives the flesh

in 12 o'clock heaven

as they step into themselves,
with eyes of light that

show flowers luminous.

For Love of Others

The more I know of love,
the lonelier I am. The more I love,
the better I am, the more I taste it, the more
it fills my tributaries, the more I am become love.

The colder I am without it,
the more the sunlight is not there, the more
I remember it, the more I wish to be "it",
and fill you, surround you.

The more I sing, the lonelier I am
to hear.
The more we become full angels,
the more deafening God's music is.

The more I speak to heaven,
the more I want my voice to be part of the
body that sings.

The more I lose an arm, a leg,
And move towards you
the more I wish me useless to myself
for you,
my loved one,

my compatriot, my world.

The Secret

Who will bury me with this secret
that makes me sing,

bury me with this heart
that is my mouth,
my grief?

Who will take me from the
goldenrod, in any season,
and show me I was?

I have leapt past my own grave
with a song like my
bones, for
all.

And when I am gone, and have stones for eyes
and my body becomes
a farewell, I shall be redeemed
for love of
the world.

A Nun Is Such a Small Thing

a nun is such a small thing,
shot several times, gone to meet her
maker; maybe she is one of the virgins waiting for
us in heaven—maybe she is a prayer of mercy
in place of justice;

maybe, as the atheists would have it, she is just a
casualty of the stupid.

maybe it is about what escapes the
fingers of accusation after ideas have had
their war—about innocence getting the
spotlight after the vanity
of men.

maybe a nun is a star in the firmament.
an offering, a sacrifice;
a dead hostage,
in the harvest of the times.

maybe she was sinful and her narrative
was replaced with myth.

maybe it teaches us to watch our words,
or to face a corrupt theology.

maybe a nun is an asterisk that was flesh and blood.
And there are many like her, and waiting in line
like us, for retribution to fall.

maybe she is what went out like
a light in the forest, by which we see now,
more dimly,
where we should walk.

such a tiny thing.

like a child in us.

Americans

I have not heard from Rudy and
Muriel in ages. I hope they made it back
safely from Mother Angelica's in Alabama,
and from Nashville; that's like them, very
American, mixing religion and bluegrass;
they're open minded about their fun, I'll give
'em that—line-dancing, fishing, though he
throws up every time he goes on a boat—can't
keep 'em down, Americans, visiting long lost
cousins in Sicily and getting by without a
word of Italian. unstoppable, birthing children,
grandchildren, promising they'll come and visit you
anytime; too busy to do anything like being still,
except to nap or sleep or cry at a funeral; for a moment—
only a moment; life goes on, by golly—try stopping
them, bellies full of hurt and pains and heads of
rummaged memories; but they'll sap life, God's gift,
for what it's worth and that's why God invented them,
I guess. I miss them, Rudy and Muriel, who met at the
Fatima Dance at the ferris wheel and lived happily
ever after, a Polish gal and an Italian
fella, going through corvettes and discos and
car shows and barbering and fishing and raising five
kids and keeping in touch with childhood this-and-that—
enjoyed every American trend for
30 years; and loving, resisting bad values and
rap, and full of home-spun wisdom, and prayerful, and by
golly happy to see you, happy to see everyone, wishing no one
harm and taking no one so seriously that they'd
get depressed by them.

I love Rudy and Muriel. Unlike my father and mother,
they brooded about nothing, maybe because they belonged in
America by three generations, maybe by faith, maybe
by just believing the American way—I don't know.
But I miss them. I want all my brothers and sisters to be like that—
careless and taking the blows, and bowing their heads on
Sunday mornings. It is always a Sunday morning
when I think of them, driving to church to say mass, as I
think of them, trying to get all my people to be like that,
to live like that, not with a hanging Christ in the arms of
a therapist, but with the good news that salvation
is taking everything that a scattering God swings likes
sparklers and stars from his heavenly hand; and
saying thank you with every fish pulled out of the
Susquehanna and then throwing it back so there'll be more—
there will always be more for them. That's their theology.
I love them, these unthinking Americans, these
civilized people.

How Not to Believe in the World

look at all the people that
will sing to you only in your sleep

who need you only when you're down and
out, the heroism that is behind
canisters and brooks,
the moonlight wasted, the coughing spell
that spells "who for".

I am behind the mean and miserable,
the voice of love that says come to me (you did
not, last time), but I have waited, looking
like heart and diamond, grist and grief.

I am the only valentine you will ever have,
everywhere, the littlest thing that you are
grateful for, the bits of universe demanding
hope from you and dishing back
a reason for your staying alive.

I am love, your eyes, the sentiment that returns
before spring, the belief in yourself that was just
an excuse for lilacs. I am everywhere and nowhere,
neither obvious nor special. I dress in no person,
but I hear your voice in every word, saying paradise.

Love's Music Harmonized

I am throwing a party with all my
ragged queens and princes, spectred,
and full of dance.

It is a party for the becoming;
all those who were beautiful to each other,
stepping into the promise of tomorrow—
that tomorrow they could never graze once,
the tomorrow we will step into like children,
holding hands, never afraid of what
we cannot be or give.

I have known love the likes of which,
unlike the poems I tried to end so well;
love that never ends,
that walks with me,

and the authors are my angels
for whom my door is always open,
and I am only in the garden,
with the trees and leaves.

Poor People

where do the poor people go?
in the city of gentrification,
in the city of buzz and excitement,
in the "creative city".

in Montreal a man is almost crushed to
death in a garbage truck because he was sleeping
in a garbage bin. this is what comes of chasing
the homeless off the streets.

extermination of the poor is the dream—
the holocaust of the witless.

the human—the mistake, is what
the city owns in its sleep.

take the children of the city away,
and the
city is a mother that will devour you.

her brood is sacred.
she will leave you with empty bistros
and condos that are tombs.

she will make you homeless
unless you find your home in another.

Silhouettes

Muriel phones to tell me
trees are beautiful without leaves
too

I feel that way

and before long I'll be the tree
she told me to look at—she sees it with leaves,
but Muriel likes to see the good in everything.

maybe this explains
the sadness of this time of year.

she says, look for the silhouette, when the sun goes
down or up,

as if I knew what time of day it was.
I figure the root and trunks must be still strong
to sprout leaves again in spring,

I confess my strength.

Muriel tells me things as I need to
hear them... memories coming out of the brush and forest
as the animals bring them,

and when I have nothing, these words, these
leaves will come
indifferently.

What I See of Forgiveness

What I see of forgiveness is what I learn to
spell like trees and cenotaphs, like bees and butterflies,
like arm, inverted, like a bit of blood longed for,
to usher from my mouth what says I love you.

There are no more wounded in my heart,
just world like target, just sun like smile, just spirit
frazzled by the awful intent,
my gizzard, skyward praying.

What I know of forgiveness is what remains of me,
I guess—what is left over of mercies,
for which I walk like gratitude, hands flailing
like a child for a snow cone.

Also what I know of forgiveness is what I must put every
day in my mouth like a tongue;

so many words is what I pray with,
but the tongue gets in the way, until I have it ready,
like a bud on a cloud,
like the dispenser of love,
this humanness.

The Sound of Shimmer

My father's old transistor radio
is itself, a piece of work
of art that is
my heart; it catches bits of
sunlight something like the way
his eyes caught the sun
on a day like this.

My mother too is in the white
explosion of the fleshed-out sun
of radiance; things like her laundry line,
and eggs frothed in the Sunday of all bells.
There are, extraordinary in the movements, uncles,
prayers and violets, highways,
a peck on the cheek.
There is no reason not to bless and be
blessed for the moment between terror
and ignorance.
That too I offer up.

I give myself to planks and fences
and dead men
I almost saw loving me.

Since I am a man who does not have children
I make legitimate sunlight of the helpless
matter of my life,

and I offer not prose, or salt shakers,
but my inverted soul and question,
answered in cupped hands and loving—
to see if I would walk into the yard
and be touched, like skin,
for blessing.

How Noble the Love of Things

His voice moves in them. How distant,
how close You are, as blackbird
rummages the trees.
How often has air just folded with
your promise
and taken shapes.

How like joy.
What I seek so resembles you
that I have learned
to spell body and movement
as arrival for you
and ideas, like tracks
in freshly fallen snow

and where others recognize a whereabouts—
I see my need for you
unnamed,
so far.

IV

The Hermit

I have learned to love the wood,
because it speaks

darkness, of things I can grapple with,
unlike the lies of humans.

Demons don't lie well.
Angels are mum, unless disturbed.
The sound of a murderer is honest,
in the wood, alone.

I am a man who
wrestles himself
like a vain glory,
waiting for
for his God
to come.

I hide
so he will hunt me
and snap me like a stick.

God came to earth
to put a claim
on me,

and
under stars I stand
and wait
to one day name him.

Easter

I have two illuminated cacti
that look
like desert things; my heart is
a flower
I have looked for in
the wilderness.

The cactus is a cross.
No one must know how beauty is made.

I have been to the desert.
I have seen mountains;

and I have seen nothing
like the way I lose my tears
to grief
and am forgiven.

Crystal Fish

how noble the love of things
and I do love them.

the cross,
the card on the mantelpiece,
the glass and frame on the wall,
the dried goldenrod in the vase,
the themes, just as they are,
happy among themselves.

I too should be like that,
happy as a crystal fish,
happy as my tablecloth.
the little Indian boy and girl inside the
snow globe,
the door I kissed to thank the house,
the badger tracks across the snow.
these things familiar to each other,
want me to join in some world like that.

what they say is:
our own conclusions are
the blessing of the day.
there are streams in the desert that say
the only desert is yourself, confused as clouds.
there is a ladder leaning against one fence.
it leads nowhere, and I will not climb it.

I am homebound today
with things that teach me cathedral.
what should I build, that I am not,
with arms and legs and breath that matches
what the trees use to nod their leaves,
what the statuettes use to have me pray.

time has stopped on a lonely clock,
at the precise moment of salvation.

Meditation in the Arbour

I too will love today the things of trees and wood that
are God, and pray that nothing is fleshed that is not
songstress,
and those few images
that warm me be as campfire
when I am blind to myself;

for His signs are everywhere,
and I am beautiful, past what I have been,
and tried to eat to make me strong forever.

Here, in the temple of plain wood
and desiccated leaves, as the world approaches
its autumn, and perfections claim the precious hours
of friends,
may my stillness be sufficient
as air and dusk falling,

that I may not be afraid for what comes and is had,
as easily as faith.

Orpheus Returns

Firstly, I don't believe in the world.
It looks like paradise
but I know heaven is in the dark, like
a lost key.
Only my words can bring it back,

like prayers,
like blind men tapping.
Finally there is the only song I had not
prepared for.

I know this, that the world is
invisible, as I look to
the centre of the earth for the grace that lines
my bones, as I wait for
something like mercy.

Love is what I would have uttered
like a song to sing without a mouth,

Love is what I wanted to hear—
Like the sound of creation praising itself.

Parish

the kid that shows up to serve the week after
his mother dies, the boy with the heart stitched shut
for the seventh time—Joe, with Parkinson's who takes
communion on the tongue.

these are my people.
they dance on clouds.
nothing can shake them, and they unshake me; they
know water passes from my hands on the way
to a gulf, a sea.

they humble me and teach me that
gifts are
no more my concoction than the day
I was born.

no death can haunt me.

my family is a stone on which
I engrave, tentatively, my name
like a keepsake.

they are with me, until
my eyes have ceased their stutter
and this heart stops beating
to anything but love.

The Walk

Walking along Clinton Street
October 2005, the houses bow down to
me at three in the morning; they say
do we remind you of other houses,
doorways left unpassed?
Do you like what is made for you?
I come from so many friends and
conversations I would have died to have
when I was 14.
I have all I want is my guess, fighting my way through
life's give and takes, loving, bleeding,
grooming my age and remembering the fine
things I love remembering.

The leaves are a cathedral that bow down; the wet patched
leaves of a winter not yet here and a summer
mulched in botched, heroic tries
at aliveness; tonight the world bows
down, leaves, stars, shingles; 'we were made for you'
the world says, now and again, as if you were
the only survivor in the holocaust of your life.
And the creator gives, sends thanks, your own,
when you almost remember everything,
life flashing before you without drowning.
This October, what is it, the 10th, the 11th, this thing
you will remember in another night like this
in heaven—or is it heaven walking between pain and joy,
a passerby? The day you were born you felt
like this, unprejudiced by kiss and want.
Maybe today is as good a time as any
to be born; the rest—a dream; some bad incarnation
that died to make you flower.

Send Me This Man

who is this new man?
he has teeth and a flag
a good man
Godsent
sure of himself
as a daisy

hero
love, all
I could want saviour

send me this man
who writes,
loves
whose zest for life exceeds me

brother
under my skin, butterfly

not my dead brother
but me
redeeming me by art
creating sunflowers where they are not

who sees heaven
where I am not
who confesses me
when I cannot

Snowless Winter

a little bird lying on
the branch beneath the window,
splayed like a winged thing,
head tossed to the side like
a rebuffed saviour.

crashed into the window, looking to find
my heart, perhaps when I wasn't home.

it makes me think of Christmas this year,
though there is no snow to cowl him,

makes me think my saviour comes, to an inn,
to my heart to my life and if I have wounded Him
with glass thoughts or the dumb heartless.

I would my house were a present,
I would I could have a place to rest
in His visiting, I wish I could have that bird fly in
again and I would open the window, this time,

like much of myself, oh grace; and though I thank
the world there is no snow, may it fall like
all these messages from His heart
to shelter us, to rest, to understand the stillness
before death, in love.

The Pastor of Them

I gave them sock and dew,
wind and blood, blessing and
restitution; they gave me absence like the
wind I was the sail of.

I came home to myself to find them
what angels thanked me of,
and loneliness like hands that
looked for me.

I am now what needs to
bless them, like a body without
speech.

Leaves, I might have been—dead leaves,
or rain cloud before sun,
or just their baptized child with a hat
of noon, and laughter that
dishevels winter eves.

What I miss of them in me,
is service, like what I am,
sprouted from the planet to
make light a stitching for
more light.

Happier in their homes,
I am what is husked, like what was
harvested to make them come awake.

Much of what I am is
their betrothal to what came of them,
from the creator's mouth.

What Then Is Grace

What then is grace, but the uninvented,
that does not come like flowers,

but like breath from the heart, the mouth, the memory
of God when all that was given is yours.

What then becomes passionate and clear?

that heaven is
will and dreams, gazebos and
coffees—
some vision of singing the mundane,

some furniture
for clouds,

some seduction of
what is beautiful.

A Place

Yes, stars and things,
trees and water.

When will you walk towards me;
When does the poem put
its clothes down?

Behind the bones there is
a constellation,
the unwritten letters that
wake up to a field of dandelions.

God is happy with so little,
really; he puts the
stars and things
there, the trees and water,
a background, for the song
he sings.

Listen, here is your life, walk towards it,
he says.
And the deaf
kiss.

Arriving at that Near Place

there is great love here, I tell you,
based on a simple need
which once I thought
kept me from being seen clearly.
It will do—his need that
I be a father, my need that she be a mother,
that a sister be here. It was our need
that held us to each other
as family, and the cry for help,
acceptable in any form.

how we have run from each other,
trying to be great.

the return to the small town is inevitable.
it was not a city. it was not glorious
in deed and word,

it was the place to meditate on, like
boys watching fish leap,
all those bright shiny fins in the
sun, and our familiar wants, our brothers.

we were so similar
because we shared a place
to meditate upon and love,
like skin walked in for a lifetime.
and the same breath, sacred;
the same wonder, shared.

And love—In all Its desperations,
welcomed.

I Love This Too

I love this too, the world,
as it comes for me, and in me
and all its paraphernalia which sounds
like the capitol of it.

I have watched dogs have at me.
and God shield me,
and thistles too by the side of the road
have sung their alarms at me,
or whatever they were glistening, and

I miss too the world I did not
make much of,
and soil,
and darts.

I am alone so, now, with big electric
lights on country roads,
and ghosts, dead relatives of my spleen
whoosh by; how do I talk fast
enough to explain anything?

I say hands, long eyelashes, a book
I did not read.
watch how my lips flap
in defiance of the stars.

look how the sky lets drop one
wide tear the size of a cityscape.

what do I want to say that is not
love me, and want me, oh wood,
with me as your brethren against fencepost
and starlight?

Moths

God like a moth,
like a baby shrine plastered on
the wall,
or like a triangle with its legs
not stirring.
Just a little to remind you
you are on the way home,
blind, like a moth to light,
blind but to heat, blind but to
the electric air.

I must not scare off these living things
that give directions.
I must be careful with sun, moon, stars.

I look at things closely. It is not wonder.
It is stories I hear of chance meetings, murders
and songs.

A long lost uncle is what I need,
but I will not take my eyes off the moth,
in mid-summer, and I will pray for
the lingerers of fall, and I am humble for
winter moths to come.
I am quiet and I wait.
For moths too must become
angels, transform, as I will,
into something with clear eyes,
that can see home.

Prayer for St. Valentine's Day

It's Valentine's Day. Everyone's on the street, hoping to be
or meet a true love. Some had it, but lost it
or their devotion to it,
seduced by rights, autonomies.

So here we are with no languages, and many,
hoping for an angel—the angel of
synchronicity, the angel of chance, the angel of luck, the
angel of providence—
any name would do;
maybe the angel of mercy.

Send someone who believes in 3rd world rights,
empowerment, gentleness and strength and nurturing; someone who
believes in romance, but won't make me scrub a pedestal—
someone with a fast car, who can build a home for my
options.

The shop windows are littered with hearts, with red, paper
hearts, with arrows, and cupids, as real as the Santa
two months ago;
oh let us believe in Santa Claus, let us believe
we are children, and not social critics of stereotypes
with raised expectations. Let us not be ourselves
for just one day.

Let us believe
that "gender" is a noun,
that irony is a poor bedfellow.

Let us believe in the fantasy that makes us real.

Let us have a love, a prince or just a wife.
Let us not have defined words into loneliness,
for just one day.

And let us encounter the passion,
and not the negotiations of love.

Spirit

I am dead to
my providing hand
that feeds nothing and no one.
I would rather it were a bird
or a way of light.

If I could release myself, only to come home.
But it is for someone else to release me,
someone other.

I may dream this. And may so many metaphors wake
like tiny ants carrying off their wounded.

I need only that this hand be a bird,
and that the doorway of your heart be open, always,
that I may return, with joy and will—

on a day that is a blessing for you.

Grazias

thank you for
the poem, the sea of the page,
and blankness of air,
and the water, not quite background
and the body just arms and legs
and not space, but heart.

thank you for another day, and trees and coughs
and leaves and musics,

and meaning
and sounds.
and the sound of sounds, and phrases

and flowers that startle

and stones and ripples

and these bones
naming themselves like love.

Wine and Roses

let me embarrass myself with tears.
let the leaves stand for time.

let food be heaven, and
a place for supper.

let everything be itself,
in the heart of the loved one.
let the past have
no diminuendo
let the seasons stop
until the hands are betrothed.

let sentimental children grow
to accomplished
kisses.

let sentiment be clothing
and
plead for
unfinished poems.

let kindness be love,
without interpretation,

and let my need go heavenwards

looking for
another.

Gift

How is it I wake
in the bouquet of darkness,
praising
my speech like a glove for your hand,

Love words with no one there.
The song and its instinct
Waking. The words,

like
a hand opening.

Afterword

by Michael W. Higgins

This new volume of poetry by the poet laureate of the City of Toronto and priest of the Roman Catholic Archdiocese of Toronto is a welcome addition to an impressive body of work. Pier Giorgio Di Cicco is a serious practioner of the art. He has a distinguished track record as a poet, urbanist, and lover. Yes, lover. The poet-priest as lover is neither a new phenomenon nor unconventional. But it does require a bit of contextualizing.

The poems in *Names of Blessing* are love songs: they speak to the heart and from the heart; they soar and lilt; they are epiphanies of affection and conduits of grace; they disclose the innermost feelings of the lover; they are unabashed celebrations of the Divine Lover.

This is not to suggest that the poems—love songs themselves—are lofty, ethereal things best left to angels and other disembodied sprites. In fact, Di Cicco is not shy of evoking the erotic, the romantic, when speaking of love. And in the process giving gentle counsel to those held captive to the twin powers of Political Correctness and Gender Politics.

> It's Valentine's Day. Everyone's on the street, hoping to be
> or meet a true love. Some had it, but lost it
> or their devotion to it,
> seduced by rights, autonomies.
> ("Prayer for St. Valentine's Day")

The poet exhorts: "let us encounter the passion, and not the negotiations of love." Di Cicco is obsessed with passion and with the loss of it. He knows that to love genuinely is to be passionate, not indifferent, detached, safe. He knows the cost of love; the price to be paid for the passionate response. In a particularly moving poem, "The Homeless," Di Cicco reminds us that the importunate panhandler, with his mad gestures, grunts and groans, is

> … God in tatters for my taking.
> He is much, and himself, whom I will never take home,
> whom God visits since I cannot love.
> He is my own shock
> at my terrible need,
> whom I cannot run away from, where once I might have;
> because I have been bedfellows with my own
> stinking grief, and now cannot scare myself away;
> and so I make friends
> with everything that looks like me,
> impoverished wonder that I am,
> with no facsimiles
> to shun.

In other words, there is no escaping the God in others, the God who elicits our love, the God who sustains us with love. And that's the point that Di Cicco never tires of making: the ineffable God is ever-present even when a hidden God, a *Deus absconditus*, a God to be searched for, to be discovered. A God full of surprises. Like the priest-singer's poetry. God is love and love is gratuitous; there are no conditions; it is pure unalloyed gift.

> the greatest things—let's have an understanding—
> are not confusing sensuality with passion,
> of love with fulfilment,
> of heaven with possibility; the greatest things
> are about belonging to what you have no command over—
> sunsets, tears, and the face that is dearest;
> love is about being killed when you lack the inclination—
> ("The Wilderness")

Di Cicco is a messy poet because he knows that passion is a messy business. He also knows that we happen upon the Transcendent in the muck and mire of life and that we taste God's beauty in the ordinariness of things. The mundane is suffused with the luminous.

And all of creation manifests the plenitude of God's tenderness. To emphasize that point, Di Cicco delights in the use of stark, sometimes unsettling, but always wondrous images and metaphors in the manner of the Metaphysicals, those English poets of the seventeenth century who reveled in outrageous conceits and disarming allusions. In "Snowless Winter," a bird that has crashed into a window is the broken Redeemer:

> a little bird lying on
> the branch beneath the window,
> splayed like a winged thing,
> head tossed to the side like
> a rebuffed saviour.

The bird/saviour, though rebuffed, is not defeated:

> I would my house were a present,
> I would I could have a place to rest
> in His visiting, I wish I could have that bird fly in
> again and I would open the window, this time,
> like much of myself, oh grace

And we are like moths drawn to God's love in the way they are drawn to light, to fire, and so extinguished. God's rapturous love can be a dangerous love if we are intent on our autonomy. Kenosis, self-emptying love, is terrible in its exacting price, but the perfect freedom:

After vocabularies, timetables,
syllables
I will like wafting snow just
drift towards you,
and obey,
not by the hand that names me but
by the wind called spirit.
("Kenosis")

Di Cicco's poetry abounds with angels, but we are never quite sure what they are because they have several meanings. They are subtle and shifting symbols that probe more than they define, suggest more than they equate. They are messengers, emanations, harbingers of love. They are a blessing; they are songs; they are poetry. And they are real.

And a poet/lover/singer for whom the real is an abstraction, for whom imagination is a paltry matter, is likely to miss the power of the insignificant, the "tiny thing," the vehicle of wisdom among the learned, so easily discounted in the order of meaning and value and yet the "child in us" that will save us. Di Cicco explores this paradox with shocking insight when he explodes the complacency and bias of those who miss the prophetic and solitary witness of the waiting virgin in "A Nun Is Such a Small Thing." Maybe she is "a prayer of mercy," "a casualty of the stupid," "a star in the firmament," "an offering, a sacrifice; a dead hostage in the harvest of the times," "an asterisk that was flesh and blood," and most importantly, "maybe she is what went out like a light in the forest." And, maybe, just maybe, she is the innocence that confounds the worldly, the "tiny thing" that is an aperture to wholeness, the radiant child that will not be mastered by the controlling adult. A liberator.

Names of Blessing is replete with epigrammatic wisdom and Zen-like inspiration. It is an entry point into the imagination and spirituality of a man, a priest, who is, in the words of his friend and fellow poet Dennis Lee,

> an intensely social animal: gregarious,
> intelligent, cantankerous, lonely, droll,
> obsessive, impulsively tender. He gives off none
> of the "stink of holiness" that spiritual
> directors warn against.[1]

Indeed, there is no "stink of holiness" in *Names of Blessing*. There is playfulness, energy, encompassing love, outrage, regret and humility. Humanity withal. And with the Spark of Divinity.

Michael W. Higgins is a professor of English and Religious Studies and the author of Heretic Blood: The Spiritual Geography of Thomas Merton *and* Stalking the Holy: In Pursuit of Saint Making.

---

[1] Dennis Lee, "Afterword," Pier Giorgio Di Cicco, *Living in Paradise: New and Selected Poems* (Toronto: Mansfield Press, 2001).